CALLE
TO ACCOUNT

CALLED TO ACCOUNT

THE CASE FOR AN AUDIT OF THE STATE OF THE FAILING CHURCH OF ENGLAND

EDITED BY
DIGBY ANDERSON
AND
PETER MULLEN

THE SOCIAL AFFAIRS UNIT

© The Social Affairs Unit 2003
All rights reserved

British Library cataloguing in publication data
A catalogue record of this book is available from
The British Library

ISBN 0 907631 99 1

*The views expressed in this publication are the authors' own,
not those of the Social Affairs Unit,
its Trustees, Advisers or Director*

Printed and bound in Great Britain by
St Edmundsbury Press Ltd, Bury St Edmunds Suffolk

Contents

	The Authors	7
	Preface *Peter Mullen*	9
1	The overall decline of the Church of England *Digby Anderson*	11
2	The decline in numbers *Robbie Low*	22
3	Why the decline in numbers *Roger Homan*	26
4	The financial decline *Tony Kench*	32
5	Decline and governance *Anon*	38
6	The liturgical and theological decline *Peter Mullen*	41
7	Disconnection: an ordinand's view *Paul Thomas*	44
8	The failure to keep the faith *Stephen Keeble*	46
9	Accommodation to secular trends *Peter Little*	49
10	The reluctance to be different *Anon*	54

11 A Church bent on self-destruction: 57
    a view from a newcomer
    Fay Weldon

12 Who should carry the can for the failure? 60
    Digby Anderson

The authors

Digby Anderson is Director of the Social Affairs Unit.

Roger Homan is Professor of Sociology at the University of Brighton.

Stephen Keeble is vicar of St George's, Headstone, Harrow.

Tony Kench is an independent business strategy consultant.

Peter Little is a structural engineer.

Robbie Low is vicar of All Saints', Bushey Heath.

Peter Mullen is rector of St Michael's, Cornhill.

Paul Thomas is a curate and was an ordinand at the time of writing.

Fay Weldon is a best-selling author.

Preface

This short book is an attempt by experienced churchpeople, ordained and lay, to comment on the present state of the Church of England across the whole range of its life and practice. We look first at the catastrophic decline in recent years in the numbers of people attending church both for regular services and for occasional offices and rites of passage. We move on next to show how the decline in congregations runs parallel to a loss of income, both from direct and covenanted giving and the management of investments. Then we comment on the efficiency of church government – what might be called the ecclesiastical civil service.

We summarise the liturgical revolution that has occurred over the last thirty-five years and note that every new set of orders of services – from Series I and II, through the publication of the ASB to Common Worship – has been accompanied by further decline in church attendance. We believe that the form and content of ordination training over this period has been and continues inadequate to fit the clergy for the exercise of their ministry. Indeed, we further reflect that there is a general failure to keep the faith and a wilful neglect of the idea of our national church.

One recommendation in the collection is that those bishops and senior laypeople in the church's government – that is, those who have inflicted their tired liberalism on the Church and presided over its continuing decline – should finally take responsibility and resign forthwith.

Our book is a series of chapters by people expert in the particular aspect of church life upon which they offered their comments. The names of some of these contributors are listed, while others have preferred to remain anonymous. They are each responsible for their own contribution.

Peter Mullen, London, 2003

Chapter 1

The overall decline of the Church of England: an introduction

Digby Anderson

Time for the bishops to face the music on the decline of the Church

There are three fairly simple facts about the Church of England today. The first is that it is in serious decline not only in membership but financially and in, for instance, its influence on schools, marriage, medicine and morals. Though other churches, for instance the Roman Catholic Church, have experienced decline on several fronts, the C of E is unique in experiencing decline on *all* significant fronts. As the author of one of the papers in this collection puts it, there are "no redeeming features". Some of this decline is quantitative, for instance that in the number of worshippers or the budget. In other cases there is a qualitative decline as when clergy dissent from essential articles of belief or the liturgy is banalised and infantilised. This decline on several fronts is particularly noticeable over the last 40 or 50 years.

Second, although its Evangelical, Catholic and Liberal members disagree over exactly what institution the Church is, they do, unsurprisingly, agree that it is an institution with a hierarchy, lines of command and authority and accountability. It follows, by implication, that someone is responsible for the decline, or at least for trying to combat the decline. The C of E is an episcopal church. Both scripture and tradition make it clear that bishops are responsible for the Church, for their flock. They may not be the only ones responsible, especially in these days of synodical government, but they are responsible.

Third, there is no sign whatsoever that any of those who might be considered responsible for the Church have publicly recognised the extent of its decline over several fronts and their own responsibilities for it. I do not recall any bishop feeling obliged to resign following the manifest failure of the modern church. Nor have any of those bishops and other senior persons, who are responsible for the many bright wheezes justified as making the church more relevant and popular, admitted the failure of and indeed actual harm caused by their wheezes, and apologised. In business, even in politics, such apologies and resignations would have been considered normal. One might have expected the church to have embraced higher standards than business especially given its frequent denunciation of it.

It is this third fact which is the most extraordinary. The alarm bell has not been sounded. More than that, there appears to be a concerted effort to run away from the bell rope and seek refuge in rosy self-delusion. What would it take to make a senior bishop say the simple truth that the Church of England is in critical decline; that grave mistakes have been made; and that, if something is not done very quickly, it will cease to exist in recognisable form in fifty years?

Instead the nearest we get to a statement which gives an account of performance and costs is the glossy *The Church of England: A Year in Review 2001-2002*. Here we see a picture of a pretty country church in beautiful condition, another of a church at Sudbury being lovingly restored, one of the Archbishop of Canterbury with the Queen, the Bishop of St Albans laughing with a nurse, one of a school with a disproportionately high number of black pupils, similar proportions of the congregation of a cathedral by a banner about asylum seekers and another showing the award winning gardens of the Commissioners. The text is punctuated with yesterday's politically correct cant about "diversity", "grassroots", "engaging", "partnership" and "outreach". Working groups are unveiled with stirring titles such as "Breaking New Ground". And the then Archbishop of Canterbury proudly claims that the C of E has "unparalleled commitment and participation in the community". He has obviously forgotten the last half millennium, at almost anytime during which the Church had more impact on the "community"

The Review does include some figures but they are arranged to show how much is being achieved now rather than how ill this compares with the past. The Church Commissioners, it is explained, have done rather well during admittedly difficult times. In short the Review paints a happy picture of a successful church. You would never guess this same church is in the worst state ever.

In other publications, when the bad news about the Church does emerge, it dribbles out. The bad news, across several fronts, does not come all at once. There is no annual audit and report covering all the fronts. The basic accounts are of course annual but most businesses, along with the accounts, give a host of details about the state of the company which links all these facts with policies pursued and persons responsible. The news on this or that front about the Church seeps out piecemeal, often not even from the Church itself. So this week there are headlines about the church attendance, a few weeks later about the disastrous state of the finances, another month later about the fall in baptisms or the decline in religious weddings. As I write this, a survey is published showing how many liberal clergy do not believe central beliefs of the Church yet still draw their stipends. There's another about the reluctance of the bishops to defend the Establishment and their peculiar place in the House of Lords.

To most of these there comes from the hierarchy of the Church no considered reaction at all. When a senior figure or body condescends to comment it is usually along the lines that things are not that bad and there are rays of hope on the horizon. A company chairman expressing such wishful thinking on the basis of such poor results would be laughed to scorn and his share price punished accordingly. The hopeful stance taken by the church hierarchy is taken as if it were virtuous. It is not virtuous to ignore huge alarming indicators and search for tiny rays of hope to compensate. When Christian theology talks of the virtue of hope, it means a commitment to faith not evasion of truth. Thus someone will say, for instance, when faced with yet another battery of figures showing decline in membership or Sunday attendance, communions, baptisms, confirmations and religious weddings and funerals, that although this is regrettable, we are getting more people to weekday services. Attendance is changing rather than declining. This, of course, is untrue. Attendance is changing but the changes do not offset the decline. The tiny increase in weekday services does not offset the huge decline on Sundays. Moreover, Sunday attendance is a Christian obligation: weekday attendance is a Christian privilege.

Even more absurd evasions include the "it's not all bad news. I talk with a lot of young people and I find in them a remarkable thirst for meaning in life". This has been trotted out at least for fifty years All one can say is that since, from the Church's point of view, the solution to their search is just round the corner at St Whatever's, either the searchers are not searching very hard or the guardians of the solutions are very successful at not being found. One of the papers in this collection shows evidence that the Church is actively putting off these young people and others "at the margins". Curiously the dumbing down of liturgy, justified as opening the door to young people, turns out not to attract them. It is the more committed who favour innovation and participation.

This tactic of trying to offset the bad news with good news grows increasingly desperate and incredible. And if this offsetting tactic is ludicrous when faced with one bit of bad news, what would it look like if the Church officials were faced with responding to bad news across all its fronts *at the same time*? For that is the question that needs to be asked. What is the reaction to declining attendance figures, catastrophic financial figures, evidence about the failure of the modern church's central worship book (it has now banned the use of the book, *The Alternative Services Book*, which, only a few years earlier it had sought to impose), evidence about the Church's failure to make an impact on national life, evidence about increasing failures to come with low participation by children, evidence about the rise of rival faiths and superstitions?

The question is not unfair. It is the same question boards of companies, headmasters of schools, hospital trusts, generals and the humblest shopkeeper have to answer, many of them annually or continually. Dr Carey as Archbishop of Canterbury indicated that he would like to see the Church become more businesslike. It is, of course, not a business and it would be silly to try to run it like a plc. But "businesslike" does not mean that. It means something much less particular. A businesslike organisation knows what it is trying to do, has clear criteria for its success and failure, persons who have power and hence responsibility for that success and failure and it applies these criteria more or less publicly either annually or when troubles loom and questions are asked. It is the plain duty of those in charge of an organisation to know the several indicators of the state of that organisation and to confront them, not piecemeal, but systematically. In the business world, leaders are not permitted to inflate the value of their shares, to conceal capital depletion or avoid making budget provision for threatening contingencies. I am not suggesting that the C of E's budget is financially unsatisfactory. But the Church is more than a business. If we look at its wider assets and liabilities, can it be denied that it is fast using up past spiritual and indeed material capital? Does the piecemeal way it informs its members of its state, really help to portray that state in the best and most "transparent way"? Why has there been no audit of the Church commissioned by the Church?

Given the Church's lack of clarity to date, such an audit should probably be carried out by an independent body. At the very least an independent body should vet it. In this short report, we try to suggest the sort of evidence such an audit should consider and the criteria it might use. The editors asked some Anglican clergy and laity to suggest headings and approaches and we print these more or less as received. Each speaks for himself and on some points they disagree. But in this Introduction I have tried to make and pull together some of what appear to me to be the key points they make, together with some points of my own.

A financial crisis

In the papers by Robbie Low, Roger Homan and Tony Kench, we see what the basic figures of decline are. The Church Commissioners used to provide, out of the central funds, for the cost of the bishops, the cathedrals, clergy pensions and two thirds of the cost of clergy (the equivalent of salaries) and housing costs. Now these central contributions to parishes have been reduced by two thirds (from £66m in 1991 to £22m in 2000) That fall is three-quarters in real terms. And clergy pensions ceased to be centrally funded beyond employment in 1998. A huge financial burden is thus transferred to the parishes. Moreover the number of retired clergy and their widows has increased by 25 per cent over a 20 year period and the cost will increase with longer life expectancy. This burden hits the parishes at a time when their attendance, that is their sources of funds, has fallen by 41 per cent (between 1979 and 1998).

A plunge in attendance

In the fifty years between 1930 and 1980, the C of E lost half of its members (figures from electoral rolls). The 1970s, the start of liberal experiments, saw 40 per cent of that decline. It slowed a little in the 1980s, to "only" 23,000 souls, rallied feebly in the early 1990s (by one person per parish per year), then plunged again in the late 1990's to 54,000 a year. This was during the great leap forward of the Decade of Evangelism. Over the past decade attendance figures fell by a quarter of a million and tumbled below the million mark for the first time

Children are the future worshippers: or, rather, in the case of the C of E, they are not. In 1991, 223,000 children went to an Anglican church. The expected figure for this year (2002) is 80,000. Infant baptisms halved between 1970 and 1990, and dropped by a further third in the 90s. Confirmations now stand at one male and one and a half females a year for each congregation. There is one figure which has gone up. There are now double the number of bishops and dignitaries than there were when the Church was more than twice its current size.

A culture of decline

The position is worse than these figures show. Consider a church which, in the early 1960s, had sixty or eighty communicants on a Sunday. When that falls to 40 or 50, the church maybe has to face the loss of a curate and some income, but it continues to behave, to look and feel much as before. Once it falls again to 30 or fewer real problems start. It can't raise enough money to pay its way. It does not have enough people to do the tasks necessary, for instance a treasurer or someone to organise evangelisation of new members in the parish. Those thirty souls are in the same large church building which may now be in manifest disrepair. Many such churches built in Victorian housing areas now enjoy the full range of problems that the inner city provides, from drunks wandering in to shout abuse during afternoon baptisms and discarded syringes in the porch, to the vicar assaulted outside or inside his vicarage. Even if they can forget the size of the place, their small numbers and their inability, despite their best efforts, to make the church and its worship what it was, are deeply dispiriting. To add insult to injury, what they get from their dioceses and the hierarchy are more bureaucratic demands, more silly new schemes and more demands for money. There is a culture of decline that goes with the facts and numbers.

The betrayal of Christian marriage and family life

As late as the 1960s the dominant ideal of marriage in Britain was a Christian one. Divorce was a minority pastime which carried social stigma and attribution of "fault". Children born out of wedlock were "illegitimate". Indissolubility was an ideal in marriage; adultery frowned on; pre-marital pregnancy a cause for scandal and often for marriage. One parent families were few and far between. Homosexuality was both illegal and stigmatised, abortion largely illegal. Britain now leads Europe in the divorce stakes. Abortion has soared. Homosexuality is legal and celebrated. Half of marriages end in divorce. All manner of what were considered perversions and infidelities are now recommended by counsellors as self-affirming.

This huge revolution has never been systematically attacked by the C of E. Bishops and other leaders have not been shy of courting publicity for all sorts of political stances but have never in any body taken a firm stance on this betrayal of the essence of Christian morality.

There is one often overlooked consequence of this betrayal which is germane to any audit of the state of the C of E. When we talk of losing or keeping members of the Church, it should be remembered that, in one sense, the Church is always losing members by death. In the past dead members have not been replaced by new converts but largely by the children of the dead members. Simply it was usual for Anglican parents to bring up their children as Anglicans, with the help of the Church, and thus numbers were replenished. It follows that any disruption to the continuity and stability of the family is, as well as being worrying in terms of Christian morality, a potential threat to church membership. As church membership falls it becomes increasingly possible that the C of E child of C of E parents might marry a non-C of E wife and bring up their children outside the C of E. Divorce and "re-marriage" carry similar possibilities. So does extra-marital cohabitation. That is why some more perceptive religious groups – one thinks of both Orthodox Jews and Roman Catholics – have become so preoccupied with, respectively, marrying out and mixed marriages. The leaders of the C of E have either failed to see the break up of the family as a threat to their own membership, in which case they have been remarkably stupid, or they have not cared sufficiently to do anything about it. Of course these trends are powerful and difficult to resist, but resisted they must be if the Church is not to be undertaking the wholesale conversion of England for each generation.

The surrender to secularism

The C of E, at its best, used to be engaged with national life but on its own, religious, terms. It helped make the wider culture. Its teaching about good and bad, about the nature of man, undergirded the courts and the law, the universities and school, medicine and nursing, welfare and charity. Its language helped mould the national language. Excerpts and ideas from its sacred texts seeped into daily proverbs and common talk.

The relationship has now been reversed. The Church is still engaged in secular and national life. Indeed it often congratulates itself on "bravely speaking out" on political matters. It is difficult to see what is "brave" about repeating liberal conventional wisdom. Moreover the speaking out is done from the utterly secure position of a safe job for life. No, the difference is not that the Church has ceased to speak on secular affairs but that, whereas it brought its own terms to those affairs and fed them, now it has a secular agenda and feeds off it.

In the late 1960s and 1970s it jettisoned its central sacred text, *The Book of Common Prayer*, a book hallowed by time and use, which itself incorporated still more distant past wisdoms, for a series of experimental booklets in more accessible language. These were followed by the imposition of a standard worship text of incredible banality. Having enforced its use, the Church suddenly banned it in order to produce yet another. The reasons for this contempt for the past, tradition and beauty were not primarily theological but political. Banal language was said to be necessary in order to speak to ordinary people, to be modern, to avoid being elitist, to be up with the latest secular obsession with minority "rights". The experiment has not worked. "Ordinary" people have not flocked in. Even by the end of the 70s it was obvious that the experiment had failed so, as with all bureaucracies, efforts towards the goal were not abandoned but redoubled.

More generally the C of E lost its nerve, its confidence to advance its own sacred truth. Instead it fell for the truths of its competitors appropriating now the terms of psychotherapy or community activism, now those of counselling or Marxism. In its rush to be as modern as possible and to speak to the latest cause it has more or less been ousted from or given up its special influence in law, medicine and the professions and its contributions to politics are indistinguishable from secular trendy rant. In some cases it has gone further than embracing secularism; it has taken on what one author calls a "butler" role. It sees its task not as advancing its own doctrine or defending its privileged position in schooling, the House of Lords and the Establishment but as acting as the servant of new communities and ideologies, trying to advance and learn from people of contrary and no faith. As with leftish intellectuals who hate and attack their own country and people, so the modern church gladly disparages its own past to advance the future of those who would once have been seen as its enemies.

Decline however you look at it

The criteria for judging the failure of a church are many. Here are a few:

Lower baptism figures; that is, figures for entry into the church
Lower confirmation figures; that is, figures for full membership
Lower communicant figures; that is, figures for practice in a sacramental church
Lower membership figures (electoral role)
Fewer church weddings
Fewer church funerals
Lower income from donations
Worsened state of central funds
Worsened central provision for pensions and clergy stipends

Dilapidation of "plant"
Reduced influence on the young at school through church schools
Reduced orthodox religious instruction
Failure to get such instruction a priority place on national state curricula
Reduced influence in universities
Reduced influence in medicine and medical ethics
Reduced influence in the practice of law
Reduced influence in the formation of law
Failure to maintain a distinctively Christian understanding in nursing, welfare, charity, youth work and in hospices
Failure to maintain Christian influence in the armed forces
Failure to contain and even discomfort rival religions and even more anti-religions such as Marxism
Failure to maintain doctrines assented to and taught over the past two millennia
Failure to maintain the texts in which these are enshrined
Failure to discipline members, especially clergy who do not subscribe to basic credal documents
Failure to maintain high standards of dignified worship
Failure to ensure that only the best of artistic culture is used in church liturgies
Failure to maintain the clergy in general as a full-time profession
Failure to make Christian marriage and family life the norm in society

No doubt there may be argument about the odd one of these and even more so of their relative importance. My point is that the Church of England has failed on all, or nearly all of these fronts. And each one of them is a matter of considerable importance. That is an outstanding achievement. Whose fault is it?

Well, of course other churches have had their difficulties too. The Roman Catholic attendance figures are not impressive and they have a severe shortage of clergy. No doubt the modern age is inimical to religion and the traditional morality which religions loyal to their identity teach. Yet other churches such as the Eastern Orthodox and some "fundamentalist" Pentecostal churches have increased numbers, the first of these with a totally "old-fashioned" liturgy, the second with an old-fashioned morality. Within churches which have lost members such as the C of E and the Roman Catholic Church, local parish churches which are liberal have lost more than traditionalist ones. And this lesson is now appreciated by Rome which is fast-tracking a translation of the Missal which will restore dignified language in the Mass.

Even if modern society is indeed inimical, if it is the enemy of religion, why has not the C of E taken it on. Enemies are best fought not hugged to one's breast and learned from. Yet a liberal agenda has subverted the Church's ability and resolution to fight the forces of decline. Even more important, these criteria are linked. If churches empty, it has something to do with what is going on in them. And what has been going on in the C of E churches for the last half century has been worship, morals and teaching to a liberal agenda. The liberal agenda was sold by those in charge because its "relevance" would keep decline at bay. It hasn't; it has hastened it.

There are three things which obviously ought to be done. Those responsible for leading the C of E into failure and decline should apologise and resign. The "policies" that have reigned during the disastrous years should be abandoned. But more urgently and in order to identify the facts and the policies and persons responsible for them, a thorough investigation is needed. The C of E has a new Archbishop. "Personally", to use his own expression, he is sympathetic to the liberalism which has caused so much damage. However, he has promised not to impose his personal preferences. He is well-placed to call for a thorough audit of the Church's parlous state and an investigation of the people and policies associated with its decline. The Church itself should commission a full, independent audit of its current state and face, rather than evade the truth.

Chapter 2

The decline in numbers

Robbie Low

It would be naive to mistake numbers for absolute truths. Like the camera they do not necessarily lie but their context and presentation can lead them to deceive. However, in any audit, numbers have their place and any organisation that prefers, as a matter of policy, to ignore the bottom line is practising self-deceit of a high order.

At national level the Church of England has devised, successively, various strategies for coping with the annual bad news that comes from the declining membership returns and Sunday attendance figures. The "Numbers are not important" strategy, gave way to a brief period of the "Those who still go are more committed" gambit. If this fitter, leaner church motif sounded too uncomfortably Thatcherite, it had a secondary drawback of being untrue. Then we had a period of total denial. The Statistics Office simply refused to issue the figures at all! Then spin took over and the current campaign of "More people come to church than you think" is to be accompanied by a wholesale revision of how the statistics are gathered. The new method is likely to make any serious comparison with previous years and decades extremely difficult. The short-term aim of preventing newspaper headlines, "Church slump continues", is unlikely to succeed. The long-term effect on domestic church organisation and planning is also unlikely to improve the lot of the poor bloody infantry, the parish clergy.

Fortunately we are still able to get a realistic picture from the pioneering work of an independent body, Christian Research, led by a former Cabinet Office statistician, Dr Peter Brierley, himself a practising Christian. Working on the reasonable premise that, if you don't know the facts you can't plan strategy, Brierley has done remarkable work, often in the face of Establishment obfuscation and downright hostility. His annual publications and updates are the most significant contribution to understanding the numerical strengths and weaknesses of all the churches in the land (as well as other faiths and cults).

CALLED TO ACCOUNT

Key numbers for the Church of England are the electoral roll (actual signed up membership) figures and the average Sunday attendance. Electoral rolls tell a strange story. Between the 1930s (the high watermark) and the 1980s the Church of England lost exactly half its membership. The disastrous 1970s was the decade responsible for 40 per cent of that decline. The 1980s saw a slowing of the downturn and an average annual loss of 23,000 souls. (The 1970s lost 80,000 souls each year.) Rolls rallied briefly in the early Nineties and showed a modest increase, until 1994, of just under one person per parish per year. Between 1994 and 1997 the average annual roll loss rocketed to 54,000 per year – not exactly what one would have hoped for in the Decade of Evangelism. Since then there has been a minor recovery amounting to one quarter of the losses incurred since 1994. But this, in itself, is what always happens between major revisions of the electoral rolls. These take place every six years and the next one was due in 2002. Statistical projections expect this to dip below the one and a half million mark for the first time and show a net loss on the last high watermark (1994) of some 300,000. While electoral rolls, pruned as they are every six years, inevitably contain some "dead wood" these figures do not seem too far off the mark. They are given greater credibility by the more immediate average Sunday attendance figures. These have slipped by a quarter of a million since 1990 and tumbled below the one million mark for the first time. This is a much faster rate of decline than the 1980s.

Even more alarming for the future of the Church are the figures for children's attendance. In 1991, 223,000 children still went to an Anglican Church. By 1996 that figure had crashed to 133,000 and projections for the current year are in the region of 80,000. Infant baptisms, which halved between 1970 and 1990, have dropped by a further one third in the subsequent decade. Confirmations have dropped to an average of 1 male and 1.5 females pa for each congregation in the country.

Other statistics which emerge from the documents include a decline in the number of parochial clergy. This may be understandable in the circumstances. What is puzzling is why there has been no parallel reduction in the number of bishops and dignitaries. There is now twice the number required by the Church of England at its most "successful" period of the 20th century. Also hidden in these figures is the change in the make-up of the clergy. Bishops anxious to reduce budget deficits are increasingly employing non-stipendiaries (private income or late middle age candidates who have a pension from a first career, cost nothing and can be trained on weekend courses). The other dramatic change is the ordination of women. One in eight Church of England clergy is now female. Perhaps unsurprisingly, the Church of England congregations have gone from a 45/55 male/female ratio in the 1980s to a 39/61 split (and widening) today. Men are leaving and not being replaced. This is disturbing for more than its obvious implications. Early research is beginning to show that the attendance of the father is a hugely more significant factor than the attendance of the mother in determining whether children, when grown, will continue to attend church regularly or at all. Indeed the gender ratio figures coupled with the horrifying slump in children's attendance and the overall speed of decline, coinciding with the ordination of women, seem to give the lie to the feminist propaganda that this particular "reform" would revive the future of the Church.

At the same time the leadership of the Church has, from "Honest to God" onward, increasingly fallen into the hands of men whose doctrinal radicalism, ethical confusion and pastoral inexperience have damaged the morale of the members and at best amused and at worst confused the unconverted. It is, for example, not uncommon to witness bishops trooping through the different lobbies in the House of Lords, hopelessly divided on moral issues.

The last 40 years have also seen the increasing centralisation of Church government and the wholesale institutional theft of parish property. Couple this to the major financial scandal of the 1990s, when the Church lost one-third of its assets, and it is not difficult to see why benefactions and legacies are no longer a reliable feature of church life. Virtually all the historic vicarages, not protected by trusts or patrons, have been sold off. The parishes, stripped of their historic assets, are in no position to defend their remaining property or their independence. Priests, increasingly on short-term contracts rather than a freehold, are understandably nervous about throwing in their lot with their parish against a predatory bishop. The establishment now speaks routinely of the diocese as the key unit of the

Church rather than the parish. It is an obvious folly to all but the careerist clergy who want to be bishops and want the bishop therefore to be managing director: a role for which he was never trained and which he is usually incompetent to fulfil.

Is there any good news? Well, some. Not all churches are declining. Some are growing. This very fact means that, as they too are part of the average statistics, those that are declining are doing so at an even steeper rate. One of the most unpalatable figures for the modernisers is the returns for the traditionalist Anglo-Catholic churches. Usually caricatured as antiquated and deliberately marginalised by the authorities, they form the only section in the Church of England that has held its numbers steady. So much so that now they account for nearly one in five worshippers; an unimaginable statistic even 15 years ago. It is worth remembering that this is from a constituency that has lost several hundred priests and many thousands of laity to Rome over the last decade and seen its remaining priests thanked for their faithfulness and success by being routinely and deliberately kept out of senior office.

Liberal churches, unsurprisingly, have declined sharply. Presumably people have taken the not unreasonable line "If you don't believe it why should we?" Even Evangelicals, overall, have suffered a slight decrease but again mainly among the liberalising tendency.

In contrast, churches that have grown as a denomination are the Orthodox and the Pentecostals. The Orthodox Church with its numinous liturgy and biblical exposition, at once fundamental and mystical, has defied cultural pressure and experienced slow but steady growth. Clearly this is not as a result of its accessibility, marketing, moral accommodation or consumer-friendly posture. Pentecostals, with their concentration on preaching and Presence, are similarly heading for a quarter of a million.

In short, people are not taken in by gimmicks. Biblical teaching and profound worship remain, as ever, the key to success. The Church of England's love affair with modernity has been unrequited. The liberal experiment is dead. Unfortunately it is in danger of taking the Church of England into the grave with it.

Chapter 3

Why the decline in numbers

Roger Homan

The Church of England has been suffering a decline that is evident on every measurable indicator. Its membership has fallen, it has closed more church buildings than it has opened; the number of its communicants has dropped, as have vocations to its professional ministry and the number of its theological colleges. The standard independent reference that gives tables of raw statistics, maps and graphs for each of the denominations is the *UK Christian Handbook: Religious Trends* edited by Peter Brierley. A more interpretative account is offered by Grace Davie in her widely cited and respected *Religion in Britain since 1945: Believing without Belonging*. It is the phenomenon of defection from religious affiliation that is addressed in this section of the audit.

Among the most instructive details in *Religious Trends* are the graphs tracking changes between the years 1980 and 2000. These are given for numbers of members (or in the case of the Roman Catholic Church, "Mass-goers"), for numbers of churches and for numbers of ministers or priests. In the United Kingdom the Roman Catholic Church has slightly increased the number of its churches but there has been a steady decline in Mass-going and in the number of its priests. The Orthodox Church has shown increases in all three indicators of between 30 and 80 per cent. The Baptists have suffered a loss of members of about seven per cent but have increased the number of their churches and have significantly attracted more to the ministry. Conspicuously, the Church of England shows decline on all three indicators: in the last two decades its membership slumped by nearly thirty per cent.

Those who need to put a spin on this consistent pattern borrow a sociological term, *secularisation*, as though to convince us that decline is endemic in the western world and that the Church of England is no different from any other Christian organisation. In fact the Church of England is very different. Its declines are singularly lacking in redeeming features and have often been sharper and can be related to particular events or changes, not least those relating to revisions in the form of its worship. The independent evidence invites at least five interpretations.

Churches offering firm teaching of doctrine and morality tend to show numerical growth, whereas the liberal churches tend to suffer decline

One reading of the statistical tables is that the congregations that are growing fastest are those that are centred on "lively" worship. Such an interpretation should be viewed with caution. Brierley's graphs are drawn on the basis of percentage increase or decline: so the new churches appear as the fastest growing because they started relatively recently from a zero base. Moreover, liveliness is not the only relevant variable: many of the new churches adopt an ultra-conservative line on some moral issues such as sexuality: it could equally well be said that people are moving away from the liberal churches and seeking firm teaching and Victorian values. Such a reading accords with the findings of Dean M. Kelley in the United States. The institutions that are showing a rising profile have in common a security in themselves that is not matched by those institutions that are prepared to follow a worldly lead. Kelley contrasts the growth of the conservative churches in North America since 1960 with a simultaneous numerical decline in ten of the mainstream churches. In the United States the appeal of churches with a conservative Christian ethic is explained in terms of their rejection of secular values; manifesting in common a sectarian tendency, they do not so much embrace worldly ways as take a stand against them.

There is a remarkable sociological insight on falling numbers in the Parable of the Sower:

They on the rock are they, which, when they hear, receive the word with joy; and these have no root which for a while believe, and in time of temptation fall away (Luke 8: 13).

The parable warns of the ephemeral nature of outward "joy" and points to the need for an appropriate grounding in good teaching. It is not a coincidence that the churches that show growth are characterised by firm and conventional teaching on the basic moral and theological questions, while the churches in decline are those that have lost their way or at least their confidence to proclaim it.

A new broom sweeps clean

In the parishes, numerical decline is associated with liturgical change. Incumbents and parochial church councils authorising "forward" changes in local usage should brace themselves for a measure of attrition. The cumulative effect of periodic leakage of one or two members of each congregation has been to diminish significantly the size, vigour and economy of the established church. In some cases losses have been considerable: in a longitudinal study of parishes in the archdeaconry of Chichester for the period 1975 to 1980, it was found that parishes changing to the modern Series 3 suffered membership losses of 14.9 per cent, whereas those sticking with the traditional Series 2 enjoyed 19.4 per cent growth.

During the twentieth century, the steepest declines were suffered in the wake of major innovations in the Church's patterns of worship

The decline in church support dates back to the years that are claimed for the beginnings of the Liturgical Movement. In the first half of the nineteenth century, church attendance rose from 18 per cent to 27 per cent and remained steady at that level until 1900, declining to 14 per cent by 1990. From the years of liturgical innovation in the 1960s until shortly after the advent of the *Alternative Service Book 1980*, the Church of England was virtually reduced to half its size.

The relationship of decline to the cycle of liturgical innovation is problematic. It could be that the Church of England is losing numbers for one or more of a number of reasons and that it would have declined even faster had it not been for the timely introduction and frequent revision of its services. On the other hand it is possible that in hoping to appeal to the spirit of the age (as perceived by itself), the Church is setting aside the very treasures that would attract its outsiders.

One of the tragic features of the Church of England is that it has ears to hear but does not hear. It listens to the language and observes the mores of the street and the office and dumbs itself down accordingly, expecting to engage people by imitating the most routine and humdrum elements of their lives. So it offers them no escape. It forgets that they have no need to come to a Church that offers them no more elevation than they already have. It misses the point that there is a mystery or magic in the Gospel and the traditional formularies of the Church and people will not come if they are not available. *Jurassic Park*, *Harry Potter* and *Lord of the Rings* have attracted large numbers not because they use everyday language and symbols but because they do not.

The evidence points to a coincidence of strategy and decline but does not prove that one is a consequence of the other. We have to take account of the fact that in the period of its sharpest decline, the Church was rendering down the language of its worship and some of its clergy, including the Bishop of Durham, were offering compromises on its fundamental doctrines. It lowered its standards and it lost its members. During the 1980s the Church of England leaked a fifth of its membership. Quite what happened in 1980 to trigger such a decline is left for the reader to speculate!

Modern services are inherently middle-class and marginalize lower socio-economic groups

For a century and more the Church's estrangement of the working classes has been recognised as one of its major failings. A hundred years ago the great surveys of *Life and Labour of the People of London* by Charles Booth and of *The Religious Life of London* by Richard Mudie-Smith dwelt upon the incapacity of the established church to attract and address the needs and sensibilities of the urban poor. These studies were quantitative without being interpretative in a scientific way: they could measure the extent of disaffiliation but they had not the means to explain it. However, in recent years Gallup and other instruments have been able to correlate factors of disaffection with demographic variables such as age, gender, region of the country and socio-economic status. At the time of the appearance of the *Alternative Service Book 1980*, the Gallup organization included in its omnibus poll a small number of simple but pertinent questions such as,

Do you prefer the traditional Lord's Prayer or a modernised version?

What kind of service do you prefer for a wedding – the traditional or a modern language alternative?

Gallup revealed a much higher level of preference for traditional forms among the lower socio-economic groups. For example, only 66 per cent of those in the top group preferred the traditional wedding service, whereas at the lower end the figure rose to 77 per cent. In response to all questions, those in the south of England were rather less fond of the traditional forms than those in other parts of the country. Even in the youngest age group (16-24 years) 75 per cent preferred the traditional Lord's Prayer and 55 per cent wanted lessons to be read in the Authorised Version. It is fair to say that polls of this kind reveal a dimension of working-class conservatism that is already well documented by political sociologists and is bound to affect the experience of the Church. We knew it already: it is not remarkable. What is remarkable – and amounts to something little short of a death wish – is that the Church has not heeded it. It has operated as though all its members were equally flexible in the face of change. And by way of salt into the wounds it has elevated from the body of its congregations a new elite who can read lessons, lead prayer, sing solo, administer chalices and assume other devolved duties leaving an underclass with no more to do than find the page and mouth the words. If the working class does stray into church, it will be disenfranchised from the word go.

So "participation" is in the practice of the Church a form of exclusion and stratification. The kinds of participation promoted in modern forms of worship are selective of the more literate. They isolate particular skills such as lesson reading, the conduct of responsorial psalms and the composition and leading of intercessions. The effect is not to generalize participation but to distinguish those who can from those who cannot. Paradoxically, forms in which the clergy and choir lead and the congregation follow are much more egalitarian within the lay body. And the point is proven too by the "new" churches, the neo-pentecostals and the charismatics whose worship is "lively"; and whose growth is without comparison in the last ten or so years; these are widely observed to appeal to the youthful and educated middle class.

Preference for traditional forms is stronger among marginal than among nuclear members

One of the more consistent and disturbing findings of recent research is that those who fall away from conventional religion or dwell on its boundaries are not less spiritually-minded but more so. Grace Davie demonstrates a decline in membership but not in faith. The sense that the Church has misjudged the spiritual condition of those to whom it would want to appeal has been recently attested by the findings of the BBC Soul of Britain poll broadcast in the summer of 2000. While religious allegiance is found to be at the level of 20 per cent, some 31 per cent identify themselves as spiritual. The belief that human beings have a soul, unfashionable though it is in the modern language services, is held by 69 per cent; and as only 25 per cent believe in forms of reincarnation, we cannot write this off as a heresy imported from oriental religion. It is evident that people are seeking support for deeply spiritual feelings and do not find this in the social and secular tendencies of the Church of England as evinced in its public profile and in the worship it offers.

Chapter 4

The financial decline

Tony Kench

Capital: from £66 million to £22 million

The Church Commissioners have a capital fund worth £4.4 billion at last report. In happier days past, the annual income from the Church Commissioners' capital was sufficient to provide for the costs of not only the bishops and cathedrals but also all clergy pensions and a substantial contribution (64 per cent as recently as 1980) to parish clergy stipends and housing costs. By now, however, the central contribution to parish ministry costs has been drastically reduced, from £66m in 1991 to just £22m in 2000; and clergy pensions are in process of ceasing to be financed centrally at all for employment beyond 1998. So what's the problem, what's gone wrong? For answers, we start with a look at (and behind) the Church Commissioners' Annual Reports.

At first sight it should be reassuring that the Church Commissioners' capital fund has in fact kept up with long-term inflation. The capital fund has grown by a factor of 3.8 since 1980 (from £1.15 billion to £4.4 billion), while the Retail Price Index (RPI) has risen by a factor of 2.46 since 1980. So in "real terms" the Church Commissioners' capital fund has actually done 55 per cent better than the rate of inflation over the past 20 years. This is not too bad in financial investment terms: not brilliant, but there are worse. To understand why there's such a serious current problem, we need to look in more detail at the income side over the last 10-15 years, and particularly to examine the pressures and trends on the expenditure side.

The income side: less available

On the income side, the well-publicised episode in the early 1990s when the Church Commissioners' capital fund lost £800m on its property investments was indeed disastrous: the value of the fund dropped from £2.93 billion in 1989 to £2.13 billion in 1992. The £800m was lost for ever, and would be worth almost £1.2 billion at today's prices. In fact it's even worse than that. If the fund had merely kept pace with inflation between 1989 and 1992, just by tracking the RPI, the £2.93 billion in 1989 should have become at least £3.43 billion by 1992, making the loss £1.3 billion (not £800m). That in turn would be worth £1.6 billion at today's prices. It would put the current fund value at £6 billion rather than £4.4 billion, and would produce a current annual income of £174m, almost £50m higher than the current actual. We will see how useful that extra £50m pa would now be.

The second problem on the income side is that during the 1990s, the rate of inflation was falling, but so were rates of return on investment. For the five years 1996-2000, the RPI has averaged 2.7 per cent pa, and the annual rate of income from the Church Commissioners' capital fund has averaged 3.7 per cent. So at a time when the church has been faced with extra costs, there has been little extra income to play with.

The expenditure side: clergy pensions

The largest call on the Church Commissioners' funds used to be clergy stipends, but since 1987 it has been clergy pensions. Clergy pension costs at £14m pa in 1980 were 24 per cent of Church Commissioners' expenditure; at £53m by 1990, they had risen to 37 per cent of expenditure; at £77m by 1995, they had leapt to 54 per cent; and at £104m by 2000 they had risen further still to 65 per cent. Even that was not enough. Another £70m has been taken directly from capital since 1998 as the first part of a seven year emergency "transitional plan", after which the Church Commissioners will cease to fund any pension contributions at all in respect of clergy employment beyond 1998, and the entire burden will fall on the parishes. In future, the available central funding will be fully committed to the rising costs of clergy pensions in respect of service prior to 1998; the total number of retired clergy and their widows or widowers has risen from 9,000 in 1980 to 11,600 in 2000, and the number will continue to rise as clergy retire earlier and live longer. It would appear there has been a significant underestimation over the years, resulting in a long-term under-funding of clergy pensions, which is now having to be corrected.

The net cost of running the cathedrals and diocesan administrations is also underwritten directly from the Church Commissioners' funds. Including all the stipends, the total was £21.5m in 2000. Costs rose steadily during the 1980s at around 10 per cent pa, but the rate of growth lessened greatly during the 1990s, averaging less than 5 per cent, and has recently been under 2.5 per cent. There has obviously been an attempt here at containing costs (and it is easy to see, too, why cathedrals have been under pressure to introduce admission charges). The total of "all other" Church Commissioners' administrative expenditure is currently £12.4m pa, up from £10.3m in 1990. It may be possible to discover some further cost savings in these areas, but they would in any case not be large enough to make much impression on the size of the overall problem of parish finances.

What is left from the Church Commissioners' annual expenditure, after the obligations of clergy pension, cathedral/diocesan and central administration costs have been met, is what's available to contribute to clergy stipends and housing, or, in post-1998 terms, "parish ministry support" is to be distributed via the new Archbishops' Council. This is where the warning flags start waving again: the Church Commissioners' contribution to parish ministry support has fallen from £66m in 1991 to just £22m in 2000: a fall of two thirds in ten years. That is a fall from what would at today's prices have been worth £84m in 1991: a fall of three quarters in real terms. No wonder there is alarm up and down the country as parishes confront the reality of having to pick up not only the great majority of the current costs of the priesthood but also its future-service pension contributions.

That drop in central funding of parish ministry costs of £44m pa since 1991 (£62m pa in real terms) would still not quite be covered even if the Church Commissioners had not lost their £800m; the problem is bigger than that. The funding of past-service pensions is consuming £50m pa more now than it did ten years ago, which alone would mop up the whole of the extra £50m pa that would now be available had it not been for the £800m debacle. So although the problem would be far less severe, there would still have to be some significant reduction in central funding for parish ministry support and future-service pensions. And, in any case, we are where we are; the past cannot be undone.

Declining parish incomes

On the other side of the ledger, to make matters worse, parishes up and down the country have been facing a long-term overall decline in church attendances. According to Christian Research's recent "Religious Trends 3", average Church of England Sunday church attendances in 1998 dipped below 1 million for the first time; they were 22 per cent lower than in 1989 and 41 per cent lower than in 1979. This has almost certainly led to declining parish incomes, although since parish incomes are not centrally reported it is not easy to be definitive about the size of the problem. The total number of paid clergy and lay-workers has also fallen, from 11,200 in 1992 to 10,100 in 1998, as retiring clergy either have not been replaced or have been replaced by non-stipendiaries. That 10 per cent reduction in the number of clergy, however, is less than half the rate of decline in church attendances. It is almost certain to mean that at parish level the financial situation is getting progressively more difficult, not easier.

Other sources of funding have been sought to help fill the financial gap. With the Church Commissioners' approval, the dioceses have been selling off the old rectories, vicarages and church lands ("the glebe") to raise cash. This started in earnest in 1978 when all glebe was placed in diocesan ownership. In the 18 years from 1978 to 1995 inclusive, a total of some £183m was raised from glebe sales (£10m pa), with about half being ploughed back into new buildings etc, for a net realised gain of some £90m (£5m pa). In the five years 1996-2000, however, the pace has accelerated hugely: a further £131m has been raised from glebe sales (£26m pa). How much has been ploughed back is for some reason no longer reported. These two decades of increasingly aggressive glebe sales represent a formula that is not sustainable for the long term: the sales have raised short-term cash but have reduced the opportunity to earn future income in rents. Selling off the vicarage to pay the vicar's salary is not a practice that can be kept up for the long term.

THE CASE FOR AN AUDIT OF THE CHURCH OF ENGLAND

The Church of England is not of course there to be a business, although it does have a requirement to ensure its future financial viability. A business consultant reporting on the Church of England as a "service business" would firstly want to consider as constructively as possible how to get the Church and its income back on to a growth path. That would involve such searching basic questions as how well it is meeting the actual needs of its potential "customers", whether it is communicating with them effectively, what greater streams of income can realistically be secured, whether the necessary skills are in place at all levels, and so on. These are difficult questions in the Church context, anathema to many within the Church, and outside the remit of this chapter.

The second consideration, however, is the one that eventually must also be faced by any business in this situation: how to reduce costs so as to remain viable within the available income. The Church Commissioners have obviously been grappling with this problem from their own point of view for some years, and doing their best to recover from the past losses and under-fundings. As noted earlier, the unfortunate result is that they are having to opt out of providing much parish ministry support at all. To quote their Annual Report for 1999, "the continuing high pensions bill and the over-commitment of our fund mean that we do not expect in the immediate future to increase the amount of parochial ministry support from the £20m we distributed in 1998".

Delegating the debts to the parishes

So the challenge of managing parish finances is being thrown squarely back at the parishes. They are now being required to generate sufficient parish income locally to cover almost the whole true cost of running the parishes, including the major part of future stipends and the whole of future pension contributions. Some external help can be sought periodically for the upkeep of the buildings themselves: public sympathy and public money can be tapped to help preserve the architectural heritage. The critical problem is the cost of the Church's own activity – the ministry, the parish operating expenses – which the Church itself must fund.

The parishes are in an extremely difficult and exposed position:

overall, congregations have been declining twice as fast as any rate of cost reduction on the Church's side. Some parishes are succeeding well in raising the size of their congregations and incomes. But in many others there is a sense of despair; not only because congregations and incomes are declining but also because they often don't know what to do about it, and can't find any useful advice. The clergy are not trained or equipped to be business managers; they tend not to have skills in financial management and financial planning. "I joined the clergy to be a pastoral priest, not a fund-raiser" is a cry heard.

It is a truism in business that you don't find out what's really achievable until you push people hard. But it is also a truism in business that it is dangerous to delegate a problem if those you are delegating it to are unable to solve it because they lack the necessary knowledge, skills or resources. The danger is that you suffer the delusion that by delegating the problem you are solving it, whereas all you may get in practice is an unwelcome surprise some time later. The problem of the Church of England finances seems extremely unlikely to be solved by simply delegating it to the parishes; the nature and inspiration of the solution, and some practical support for its implementation, must surely come from the leadership.

Chapter 5

Decline and governance

Anon

The Church of England has, for much of the twentieth century and now into the twenty-first, had four main institutional centres. These are the House of Lords (where the archbishops and senior bishops have seats), Lambeth Palace (the London home, and chief home, of the Archbishop of Canterbury), the offices of the Church Commissioners at No. 1 Millbank, and the offices, first of Church Assembly and now of the General Synod, at Church House Westminster. The Church Commissioners have an independent existence, having been created by an Act of Parliament which merged Queen Anne's Bounty and the Ecclesiastical Commissioners. Church Assembly and the General Synod combine with an elected House of Laity, independent of the House of Commons, where laity of the Church of England was represented until 1919. Three of these four centres are at Westminster, and Lambeth Palace is only a short walk away along the Thames.

In addition to these, there are of course the diocesan offices of the forty-three dioceses, and various other diocesan agencies. There are also interdenominational agencies like the National Society and Churches Together in England (formerly the British Council of Churches). And there are international Anglican agencies, like the office of the Anglican Consultative Council. But of purely Anglican agencies, directly concerned with the Church of England, the four we have mentioned in and around Westminster are the most important.

Of these four, the only one that obviously maintains an ecclesiastical "civil service" is the office of the Church Commissioners. The bishops in the House of Lords are doubtless provided for by the facilities which the House of Lords offers to all peers. But Church House Westminster and Lambeth Palace have also, each of them, a significant civil service of their own.

To speak of the Church Commissioners first: as everyone knows, early in Archbishop Carey's primacy, it became apparent that, by disastrously rash investment policies, they had lost about a quarter of their assets. The disaster had really happened towards the end of Archbishop Runcie's primacy, but it did not immediately become public. The result was that the amount they were able to contribute to clergy stipends (which in 1975 had been three-quarters of the total) had to be drastically cut, and it has since been further squeezed by the ever-increasing bill for clergy pensions, and now stands at perhaps one eighth. The problem was further compounded by two decisions taken by the General Synod in 1975 and 1976. In 1975, to meet a shortage of posts for younger incumbents, they introduced compulsory retirement. Almost immediately, the church was faced with a shortage not of posts but of incumbents, but the Age-Limit Measure has never been amended, and has further resulted in an enormous pensions bill. Again, in 1976 the Synod passed the Endowments and Glebe Measure, transferring the ownership of all parochial endowments to the Church Commissioners. Putting all one's eggs in one basket is always rash, and now that the Commissioners have dropped the basket, the parishes have no resources to fall back on. They are being told that the Commissioners can no longer pay either the stipends or pensions, and that they will have to find them both out of current income.

The Secretary General of the Synod and the numerous staff of Church House are another branch of the ecclesiastical civil service, and can take many initiatives, sometimes of a distinctly undesirable kind.

After the General Synod replaced Church Assembly in 1969, it attempted to bring all official church agencies under its aegis. The Liturgical Commission ceased to be the *Archbishop's* Liturgical Commission. The Council on Foreign Relations, which had operated quite effectively from Lambeth Palace in maintaining liaison with churches in foreign countries, was dismantled. And the appointment of bishops, which at least up to Archbishop Fisher's time had operated in quite a homely way, by the Prime Minister consulting the Archbishop and his own Appointments Secretary, and then making a recommendation to the Monarch (which was occasionally vetoed), was replaced in the late 1970s by the establishment of the Crown Appointments Commission, effectively a sub-committee of the General Synod. The Archbishops now have their own Appointments Secretary as well, and though the diocese in question has a formal voice, the two secretaries seem to produce the shortlist between them, and the appointee is more often than not a member of the Synod, of "Open Evangelical" or "Affirming Catholic" outlook.

The Boards and Councils of the General Synod have their own permanent, paid secretaries, who have much more time to work on intended reports than any elected member, and may often share the outlook of a past regime. They are well represented on the new 'Cabinet' of the Church, the Archbishops' Council. Their reports tend to be published before they are discussed, and are taken by the media to represent the mind of the Church more than any subsequent debate. The "cohabitation" report, which the Archbishop even condemned when the debate came, is a good example.

At Lambeth Palace, though stripped of some of its former agencies, a greatly expanded staff has taken their place. Archbishop Coggan dealt with his own correspondence and wrote his own speeches. But Archbishop Runcie was notorious for employing speech-writers, and also invented the "Bishop at Lambeth" as his head of staff. Dr Carey inherited a good many of his predecessor's appointments, and made some astonishingly unwise appointments of his own. He has surrounded himself, even more than before, with a secretarial staff charged with fending off enquirers, a staff who in some cases seem to be remarkably ill-informed and inept, sad to say.

The Civil Service has the reputation of running the affairs of state according to its own pragmatic ideas, regardless of what Government is in power. How far this is true of what we have called the ecclesiastical civil service would bear closer examination, but he would be a rash man who denied that there was any similarity.

Chapter 6

Liturgical and theological decline

Peter Mullen

Sometime in the swinging sixties, the Church decided that it would be a good idea to rewrite its liturgy in order to have words that would be seen as "relevant" and "meaningful" to a generation turned on to The Beatles and the recently unbanned *Lady Chatterley's Lover*. The modernisers formed a majority in the hierarchy, but in those days there were still a few traditionalists among the bishops – Evangelicals who clung to *The Book of Common Prayer* and the Thirty-nine Articles and Catholics who used the English Missal or the Interim Rite – so those who craved change were obliged to proceed with stealth.

The new *Series One* and *Series Two* booklets maintained traditional language, and in them change was confined to structural tinkering and a small number of pedantic alterations, such as the change from "in earth" and "them that" to "on earth" and "those who" in the Lord's Prayer. In 1970, Parliament gave the Church permission to alter its words for worship and doctrine and, for all practical purposes, the new General Synod became the governing body of the Church of England. The majority of innovators in the Synod – who always despised *The Book of Common Prayer* – felt they could now afford to be much bolder and introduce what they referred to at the time as "contemporary English". "Thee and thine" became "you and yours". *Series Three* was the crucial break with the words of prayer known by heart by English people for four hundred years. The oral tradition of common prayer, words hallowed by time and use, was thus broken at a stroke. The modernisers were pleased by this because, of course, any sense of historic continuity is the biggest obstacle to radical innovation.

In 1980, the massive changes in public worship produced in these booklets were consolidated in *The Alternative Service Book* (1980) – an enterprise which the Synod advertised as "the greatest publishing event in four hundred years". The most significant consequence of all this liturgical revision was that every time a new

Order was introduced, congregations declined. An auditor or a management consultant would doubtless conclude from this distressing fact that revision should be stopped forthwith. Instead the Liturgical Commission continued to turn out more and worse, and the flight from the pews accelerated. An especially evil result of the new Babel of words for worship is that our generation of children are the first to know no prayers by heart. They know none of the numinously powerful biblical passages by heart either: for *The Authorised Version* has been discarded in favour of a score of inferior and frequently inane versions such as *The Good News Bible* – a title which ought to be reported to the Advertising Standards Authority.

But the so called "modern" language is not modern at all. It is a mixture of sham antique and bogus contemporary. Anyone who has even half an ear for what will go into English knows that you can't say, "We praise you for your glory" – without sounding ridiculous. For the words "praise" and "glory" belong in the same register as "thee" and "thou". The same goes for all those other old words such as "king" and "majesty". They simply will not sit easily beside all the new egalitarian waffle about the "president" and the "inclusive" language which does not allow us to make any difference between the sexes. *The Book of Common Prayer* originates in a politics which is closer to the theocratic state – one people, represented by the monarch, under God. It is not possible to change the politics to one which is semi-secular with a bias towards universal rights and egalitarianism, *and at the same time* to retain so many old words, without a profound loss of meaning amounting to a descent into incoherence.

"The greatest publishing event in four hundred years" did not prove to be at all durable. After a mere twenty years, *The Alternative Service Book* was banned from use by the Synod and replaced by *Common Worship*. Banning books is a strange pastime for the modern church whose leaders exalt themselves so much in their praise of "democratic rights". Where now are the democratic rights of those who in good faith bought copies of the ASB in 1980? This newest of the new books takes religious utterance to such an abyss of banality that its most likely effect is to reduce the already massively dwindled congregations to nothing, or next to nothing.

Phrases such as "Let them be tender with each other's dreams" *(Common Worship Marriage Service)* and "In the same night that he was betrayed he had supper with his friends" *(CW Eucharist)* are either risible or blasphemous or both.

There is a terrible illiteracy, of theology as well as language, in the highest counsels of the Church. Even *Common Worship* is not dumbed down enough for that new Star Chamber, the Archbishop's Council which has issued instructions to every parish priest on how to download from the Internet willy-nilly, bits and pieces from *Common Worship* and then stick them together in whatever order best tickles the individual incumbent's whim. The result is that it is now impossible to find the same service in any two parish churches in the land. The authorities have thus abolished any sense of *communion* in the Church of England, where the custom is not now "all the realm shall have one use" but "every parish shall do as it likes". This is effectively to destroy historic Anglicanism and to replace it with a cut and paste, pic 'n' mix world of near infinite choice: the very model of the post-modern chaos which has so fragmented the secular world to which the church *ought* to be offering something more spiritually sustaining.

If *Common Worship* is banal, the new guidelines for worship are abject. We are told that in devising our forms of service, we must endlessly rewrite and paraphrase into a sort of baby language. So Compline becomes "Night Prayer" and Confession is "doing the dirt on ourselves". Because "O Lord, open Thou our lips" is thought to be so archaic and incomprehensible, we should paste at the beginning of our service, "We say 'Hello!'". That such instructions should come to us authorised by the Council of the Archbishop of Canterbury unfortunately says all that needs to be said about the mind of the contemporary Church of England.

If, as seems likely, the Church of England should die in the first decade of the twenty-first century, we shall not have to look very far to find its killers.

Chapter 7

Disconnection: an ordinand's view

Paul Thomas

There is a species of person called a "Modern Churchman" who draws the full salary of a beneficed clergyman and need not commit himself to any religious belief

Evelyn Waugh, *Decline and Fall*

Experience as an ordinand has not won me over to thinking that the contemporary Church of England has the courage to confront and expose society's secular inanities. Why? The Church is too firmly anchored to the secular experiment.

A supercilious Christian modernism has arisen, which is culturally arrogant, claims now to stand outside the Christian centuries, disdainful and shameful of our history and experience as Christians. Truth is determined by "context". Primitive has become a dirty word. It is a disposition which disconnects our witness from that of eternity.

What are the theological colleges and courses doing in the face of this? Little. In many parts of the Church, the programme of secularisation is well on the way in methods and manners.

One soon learns in modern theological training that tradition is inhibiting, and all precedents are there to be upturned. Little is the question asked, "How do my thoughts measure against the wisdom of the Christian centuries?" Rather "experience" is the new dogma of the Church, and any passion for the gospel which displays love and learning is regarded by colleagues as eccentric and specialist. Theological method as a result becomes conspicuously anthropological and thereby self-flattering: "How do you *feel* about this?" Please do not mention the Fall as it only gets in the way of uncritical affirmation. Transfiguration and Redemption – through Grace the potential for all humanity – are characterised as "concepts" (not realities), too lofty for the laity. Through the emasculation of Traditional Christianity, sermons have become entertainment within the liturgy, anecdotal and clichéd.

CALLED TO ACCOUNT

Ancient and hallowed forms of prayer and praise were the first casualties in this process, and they have found themselves sidelined at best, at worst condemned to outer darkness in favour of tedious novelty. Little time is found to ground ordinands in classical Anglican divinity in all its variety and richness, yet it is found for Pastoral Psychology – a discipline which types our humanity and makes Christian compassion and common sense a science.

In so many areas a distinction between thinking and feeling has emerged – between theology and spirituality. Theology has to a great extent lost its connectedness with the liturgical life which is its *raison d'être*. So too has "spirituality". "What is your spirituality?" you will be asked, as if it were a private possession and not the *Common Prayer* of God's people. What most people mean by "spirituality" is really individualistic piety. Disconnection runs deep.

So much of this condition has arisen from the cult of the Self, which the Church, whilst often criticising publicly, has done little to counter in its training colleges. Christ's ministry in and through humanity is called "my Ministry". Likewise, God's call to service is "my call" not His. The Divine love affair with humanity has been jealously cut up and claimed by individuals. What is conspicuous is a lack of wonder and awe about what is being done to the *World* which lies beyond "me".

Church authorities have forgotten that Anglican dynamism is rooted deep in the symphony of tradition: *The Book of Common Prayer* (always intended to be a book which binds people), English Hymnody & Fathers of all generations, East and West. We must plug into Unity again. The symphony has been radically disrupted by unrestrained personal choice, and has led to a confusion of identity and direction in the life of the Church which impacts upon the nation. It is a great and lasting sadness that, in so many of its parts, the Church of England has bowed to secular consumerism, offering a public what it wants, not what it needs, whilst in other parts it has hardened in a way uncharacteristic of Anglicanism.

I pray we can re-learn how to surrender to Adoration, and not Self-Satisfaction.

Chapter 8

The failure to keep the faith

Stephen Keeble

The failure to keep the faith is the common theme of nine trends in the modern Church of England:

1. The increased ignorance among ordinands and clergy of classical Anglican theology.

2. The consequent absence of a distinctive Anglican theological method informing Church of England deliberations and practice.

3. The impossibility of understanding the theology of the 1662 BCP, which officially is still uniquely authoritative, without such a grounding. All the above points were articulated in Gareth Bennet's 1987 *Crockford's* preface:

Clergy without a sense of there being some authority in the historic experience of the Church may well come to think that theology is the latest fashionable theory of theologians.

4. The now near-universal modular system of higher education brings an increased likelihood of a fragmented and distorted perception of distinctive theological issues and perspectives. Rather than being read within a context of their overall thought, thinkers are more likely to be superficially encountered in general surveys of specific subjects. This militates against any apprehension of a systematic or coherent theological understanding.

5. The ordination of women priests and the impending phenomenon of female bishops are clearly inconsistent with the historic Anglican understanding of the catholicity of the Church of England. The C of E, however, does not require its members to recognise the status of female priests and allows traditionalist parishes the pastoral oversight of traditionalist bishops. In order to accommodate this

constituency after the introduction of women bishops, the idea of a non-territorial third province in addition to Canterbury and York has been mooted; something which Archbishop Rowan Williams has recently said he is regarding "with some sympathy". Instead of focusing its energies on the pursuit of that unity of the Church for which Jesus prayed "that the world may believe", the C of E seems set to continue with a further divisive innovation contrary to the explicit teaching of the New Testament itself. It remains to be seen whether the hitherto much vaunted Anglican comprehensiveness remains capable of including those whose beliefs conform to the historic teaching of the Church of England.

6. The consequent damage to ecumenical enterprises involving the Orthodox and Roman Catholics. Much time, effort and hope have been lavished on these over the years and clear warnings about the grievous consequences were ignored. How can the C of E not be regarded as having acted in bad as well as misguided faith?

7. The loss and marginalisation of talent both clerical and lay following the ordination of women priests. It is estimated that in connection with this, the C of E has lost in excess of six hundred priests since 1994. The number of laity who have left will have been much higher. Their decision may have been influenced by Archbishop George Carey's description of those who continued to hold to what the Church had always taught as heretics, even if he did subsequently withdraw the remark.

8. The growth and power of the "open evangelicals" and "charismatics" within the C of E. Believing themselves to be conservatives, in some ways they most resemble modernist liberals. Scripture has ceased to occupy the authoritative position it once enjoyed among such Anglican evangelicals. Although directly untouched by the great religious thinkers of the past two hundred years, they have become liberal protestants, their indifference to culture notwithstanding. Unlike their evangelical forebears they are keen, if slow, followers of secular fashion. They are thus unwitting contributors to the doctrinal and liturgical drift in a C of E which has lost its bearings.

9. The widespread predilection within the C of E for the trappings of tradition unencumbered by the beliefs which engendered them. Thus in a recent survey conducted by Christian Research into "The Mind of Anglicans" only 53 per cent of Anglican clergy affiliated to the influential grouping "Affirming Catholicism" were able to affirm belief that Jesus died to take away the sins of the world, 35 per cent belief in his bodily Resurrection and 21 per cent in his unique Incarnation.

Having a form of godliness, but denying the power thereof, from such turn away.
II Timothy 3:5

Chapter 9

Accommodation to secular trends

Peter Little

It is over sixty years since I was baptised, and my overwhelming feelings about the effects of the changes which have occurred in the Church during the intervening period are of sadness and disappointment. First we should ask, what are the primary reasons for the existence of the Church? Prominent among these must be the following: to act as a secure repository and guardian of religious truth; to oversee the safe refinement of that body of truth insofar as particular demands make reinterpretation necessary for today's world with today's problems; and to attempt to ensure by proper teaching that Christians have an authentic understanding of their faith.

We are experiencing a huge dereliction of these duties. The Church has permitted an internally-brewed climate of doubt to develop over doctrine which has combined catastrophically with a growing popular misconception that all our problems can be solved by the modern and far more reliable religion of science, technology and medicine. This latter has the huge advantage of making us the victims of a large proportion of our troubles. The Church has enthusiastically followed social fashions with the general attitude of trying to be all things to all people; fashion has been followed to a degree which makes it appear that the greatest sin of all is to present judgements in case anyone takes offence. In our "liberal" society, everyone's opinion is equally valid, irrespective of the quality of that opinion; and the very word "quality" arouses howls of protest because it is the sign of "elitism". It now seems that Christian love, at least insofar as the public pronouncements of our clergy are concerned, consists primarily in being merely nice to everyone. It is acceptable for the clergy to offer opinions which undermine and lead to the relentless unravelling of basic Christian doctrine, but woe betide them if there is any hint of adverse comment about other faiths. There was a superb example of meaningless prevarication on Radio Four recently: one of our archbishops was (twice) asked a direct question about a topic of particular current ethical interest. An answer with any content was of course bound to cause offence in some quarter, and we were treated instead to a completely evasive statement about the archbishop's "excitement" about a forthcoming meeting of "scholars" which was to discuss interfaith dialogue. Such vacuous general statements cut no ice with anyone and merely make the Church look very silly. Everyone, not only the archbishop, is opposed to sin in principle, but we ought to be able to look to our archbishops as men with the discriminatory ability to make meaningful statements about sin in particular. But that requires an authentic and hard-won dedication to the study of what our religion is about.

The loss of confidence

To those for whom religion means anything, it must be true that by its very nature it is the most important aspect of life. That does not, of course, mean that the secular life is unimportant; it is supremely important in the sense that we are actually here and live out our lives in the real hard world of space and time and matter, and that even our religion must be expressed – incarnated – by fleshly means. There was a time when the clergy could be relied on to offer reliable advice to those who approached them for help in dealing with the burden of personal guilt about sin. But nowadays the clergy rarely speak about sin for fear of seeming to insult their parishioners. Quite simply, the Church has lost all self-confidence concerning what it stands for. Social problems are to a large degree the collective result of personal problems and misdirection, and it ought to be a primary function of the Church to give spiritual guidance of the highest order to those floundering with the apparent meaninglessness of life in much of our society. The tragedy is that the best minds of the two millennia of the Christian era have devoted themselves to the eternal problems of human existence, but there is little enough sign of the clergy being sufficiently familiar with this treasure-house of accumulated Christian wisdom to offer advice which will really help. Instead of sound spiritual advice we are more likely to be treated to "suggestions" based on recent fashion or, more likely, handed over to secular counsellors or psychiatrists whose advice is derived from secular humanism. Primary among our vicar's concerns will of course be the necessity to avoid discussion of the fact that our own wickedness is close to the heart of our personal disorientation; too frequently he looks for external social causes.

Silence about abortion

Given the Christian doctrine of Original Sin (and even any reasonably objective secular view of humanity) it is clear that human decadence is a fairly constant feature in any society, but as we are given the ability to reflect on this disagreeable aspect of the world it ought surely be the Church's duty to seek the remedy which is the redemptive work of Christ. Let us look at one notable aspect of decadence in modern society which is now widely seen as simply a part of the way things are. Abortionists now detach about one hundred and seventy thousand unborn babies from their mothers' wombs each year in Britain, and send them off for incineration. If this is not an indication of one aspect of society's life having sunk into a particularly nasty form of decadence then it is difficult to admit that the word "decadence" has any meaning at all. After some initial huffing and puffing, what do our Church leaders do – when they are not preserving a resolute silence? They hide (like true pseudo-scholars) behind obviously futile discussions about the age after conception at which a human being with a soul can be defined as coming into existence. And so the carnage goes on while modern churchmen avoid saying anything "unchristianly" critical about what is going on. And this despite the fact that Anglican as well as Roman Catholic teaching forbids abortion in all cases.

Changes in litany and music

Part of the Church's sad state can be attributed to the fact that, in a literal sense, it has ceased to speak with one tongue. We can now hear liturgies permutated in so many different ways according to personal taste that it is simply baffling; the particularly fruitless liberal principle of allowing everyone to have a crack at saying things the way they like them produces a destructive confusion. Leaving aside the crucial question of the quality of language (for we must respect the fact that these words are not allowed in the liberal agenda), we have during a period of much less than my lifetime lost a common religious language which provided people with that wonderful library of words which (sometimes sleeping below the surface of the mind) rise up to guide and comfort us in times of trial. Let us at least be grateful that our liberal Church modernisers cannot get their hands on the great tradition of secular literature bequeathed to us; yet they have managed to vandalise religious language to such an extent that a whole generation of people has suffered the withholding of a common form of expression of those things closest to our hearts. Instead we have an ever-changing mishmash of words, which in their great variety cannot by definition stick in the memory. This is an incalculable loss, for a person with no words lodged in the mind has no firm spiritual hinterland. The inference is that we can somehow hold a generalised idea of truth, provided that our feelings are "loving and compassionate". How am I, rooted in Original Sin, supposed to accomplish this? The whole process is badly mistaken, but it complies with the liberal agenda that anything like learning by heart is (terrible word) indoctrination. Liberals do not believe in doctrine, they make it up as they go along; except of course their own agenda, the origins of which form an interesting parallel.

The signs of the Church's following of social fashions are nowhere more evident than in the style of its music. There is a fear amounting to panic among churchmen that they might appear old fashioned. They are determined to be part of the pop culture because they neither wish to seem "elitist" nor to have any shadow of doubt cast across their pretensions to solidarity with current tastes, however decadent. Who has not walked past a church reverberating with the banal repetitiveness of the disco?

To people at large the liberally-dominated Church looks increasingly like an ineffective teacher in front of a class of children; real children, naughty, boisterous, lively and with huge potential. All manner of dumbed-down ways of attracting the pupils' attention have been tried. But the fact is that the choice of words (and music) determines what is being said. The medium is the message. And the voice of authority and authentic teaching is absent, so the children go home empty-handed and empty-headed, their sensibilities undeveloped, their ignorance of the real content of the Christian faith complete. Instead, senior clergy issue vague, flesh-creeping slogans: "meeting challenges"; "celebrating our faith"; "nourishing experiences in an informal and friendly atmosphere"; and of course, "sharing". It's like the sound of wind leaking into a vacuum.

Chapter 10

The reluctance to be different

Anon

On almost every front, the Church lacks the ability, willingness or courage to be different. It is afraid to be different, on the grounds that being different is being divisive. A neologism for this might be *diaphoraphobia* – fear of being other: *homoiophilia* = desire to be the same. This underlies so much of what church leaders do.

How has this development come about? Once upon a time, the Church of England was, or acted as if it was, just that. It maintained a healthy, at arm's length distance from Roman Catholics and Nonconformism, deploring them where necessary, converting them where possible. As the national church, it had little compunction in defending and extending its own empire – numbers, schools, mission, liturgy, and doctrine.

In the last thirty or forty years the C of E has become, in our political system of Minoritocracy, about the only minority dedicated to denying the validity of its own history, values and future – on the tacit belief that as the national church (even if residually) it should do nothing to counter or censure *any* other minority, whose gibbering totalities, they claim, make up The Nation.

It is as if the institutional memory of actually once being the church of the nation is now felt to be best expressed by going along with the idea that the nation no longer exists. So in the interests of pluralism and non-exclusivity, the C of E has become bland and mute, pathetically anxious to please – anyone, anything.

The Church of England has not so much gone from being the national/established church to being a secular lobby. It has gone from being the national/established church to being the only lobby in the land which does not lobby for itself. It has become the national butler, concerned to ensure nothing more than a formally correct welcome to any guest who presents for entry. For example, there exists the particularly scandalous refusal to take back Church Schools. One bishop said that the reason this was rejected was because it would "set the Church apart". The same attitude prevents even the teaching of Christian doctrine in church schools. The same goes for the "reform" of the House of Lords where no voice at all was raised among our bishops in defence of their own right to sit in the Lords; only a lot of shame-faced mumbling about the "necessity" to get rid of most of themselves and replace themselves by assorted Moslems, Hindus and Rastafarians – all of whom can be relied upon to press their own interests assiduously.

Clearly, a lot of this is tied in with the C of E's manifest destiny in insisting on being "The Host Community" – again, acting in this ghostly sense as the national butler, welcoming in and ushering in to our society all sorts of alien creeds which, no matter how many virtues they have, *are not and never will be either English or National*. On nearly every Community Relations Council, you will find Anglicans, often ordained, busy going to Mosques and Hindu or Sikh weddings or funerals or festival days, Uriah-Heeping their way into the social life of these other faiths by in effect relativising their own; seeking always to find some "common ground" where, fundamentally, none exists – as these other faiths keep telling them!

Again, the ghost of being "the nation" seemed to find in Lady Thatcher's re-mobilisation of the economic strength of the country a reason for being ashamed rather than proud. The General Synod's Board of Social Responsibility had long since dallied with the Gucci-socialism of *The Guardian* – as materialistic a world view as any – but seemed unable to get into its head the simple fact that "the poor" they were so concerned about stood a better chance of being fewer in numbers in capitalist societies than in any other. Such a proposition was dismissed as "materialism" or "triumphalism" or "western" or "ethnocentrism" by church leaders unable to accept or even see that what Lady Thatcher was offering was what "the poor" themselves could very readily see as the best answer to their problem.

Over the next several decades the crusaders for the "relief of Third World Debt" will surely come to see that whatever short-lived relief may be experienced by the recipients of our largesse will be overwhelmed by the moral and economic corruption to which all free gifts lead. In this debate about "the third world" can be found yet another of the ghostly legacies of the C of E: its association with "Nation". This has become synonymous with being selfish, backward looking, vision-limited. It is a strange logic which makes church leaders support national liberation movements in the third world, while insisting that we ourselves must cease to be a nation – or a national church.

Equally part of the "Host Society" was and is the C of E's response to AIDS. Where have we heard a Church leader say the obvious: that AIDS is another venereal disease like gonorrhoea or syphilis, acquired like them in perfectly obvious ways, and avoided like them in ways which are just as obvious – through chastity, fidelity, marriage, keep your trousers on – things which have been boringly standard Christian teaching for centuries. AIDS "victims" have, like the poverty-stricken dwellers in the third world, had their numbers added to by the very tolerance of their behaviour espoused by their "supporters".

A parochial note: Christians in the Northern Region could not believe it when the Church Commissioners got rid of their holdings in Newcastle's Metro Centre, one of Europe's largest and most profitable shopping centres. Why should church members, in their alms and giving, be willing to pay more and more for such incompetence?

As Church leaders are usually somewhat behind the fashion, matching yesterday's fad to tomorrow's zeal, it will be some time before its leaders wake up to the fact that the world has already passed them by and very much wants to retain the traditions, presence and credal forms which they have so incompetently wasted.

Chapter 11

A Church bent on self-destruction: a view from a newcomer

Fay Weldon

To a newcomer to Christianity, as I see myself, the Church seems bent on self-destruction. Those who run it are either, if you look at them kindly, sinking under the weight of their own empathy, or at worst, are guilty of an actual plot to bring it to its knees. When I discover that the Church is in future no longer going to employ priests, but will oblige them to fund themselves as best they can, (while no doubt enlarging its management base) I am inclined to think it is the latter. The simplest solution seems the most likely – that someone somewhere is actually trying to destroy this institution. The Church, as congregation's link between the material and the spiritual world, loses its power. Its priests, no longer relieved of worldly worries, must now dwell wholly in the material world, not act as a mediating power between God and man. This seems to me to border on blasphemy.

Now, short of an actual evil conspiracy, look to an accumulation of folly and wishful thinking for the plight of the Church. The belief that everyone is as "nice" as you are. At the root of the unease is the ecumenical movement, which suggests that nobody is "right" about religion, but that all faiths are equally valid, and worthy of the same respect. (Yet if I had been persuaded by the Islamic faith I would have joined Islam. I was not, and did not. I take offence when it is suggested to me that I might as well have.) Teach children comparative religion in the schools and you instantly undermine faith. If this religion is as good as that, and is as unlikely as the other, why believe anything at all? Faith becomes a matter of the rituals you favour, and the answer to that is, for the most part, none. No time, too busy earning.

Better to teach no religion at all, than to teach all. To criticise other religions is not to be racist – it may even be the Church's duty, an insult to its faith, not so to do. But the fear of being so labelled seems to have driven all common sense out of the Church's head.

THE CASE FOR AN AUDIT OF THE CHURCH OF ENGLAND

And as for Prince Charles – he seems to be so pro-Islam the Church might well wish to disestablish itself in order to keep its distance. The Church has driven itself into a pious, helpless, hapless corner by its own carryings-on. Canterbury now needs a turbulent priest, thundering, not mewling, dangerous, righteous.

The politicisation of the Church, resulting partly from the rise of militant gay clergy, male and female, to whom the Church is seen as a promising career rather than in terms of belief and vocation, has done it no favours. Women priests are already *demanding* to be bishops; but such management jobs should surely be taken on out of duty, even reluctantly in "someone has to do it – I suppose it had better be me" mode.

The non-aspirational, down-with-elitism mood of the moment amongst the public is encouraged by the Church's immoral and ineffectual attempts to be popular. It has allowed the happy-clappy brigade to snatch the sacrament and run backwards into self-hypnosis. It confuses "ratings" with the spreading of actual faith, and doesn't even get the ratings anyway. The more it courts popularity at all costs, the less moral ascendancy it has. It has joined the media: anything for an audience, and misreading and insulting its audience as it does, results in the audience just switching off. The Church has its Pram Service (careful here: no one has prams anymore, they have buggies) in the same way as the BBC puts on *Casualty*; those who do so know it's garbage but it gets the audiences – at first, then it loses them dramatically. There is no long-term thinking. The Church should be looking for the highest common denominator not the lowest common factor: it should be leading, but it has got into the habit of following.

The changing prayer-book unsettles people: they like to think of themselves in church as part of an ongoing tradition that has been and will go on. They want to belong to the Faith of their fathers (and mothers), and they're not allowed. They soon enough settle, however, because it is gratifying that so much effort has been made on their behalf, and it *is* easier not to struggle for understanding. At the same time they investigate the new text and find nothing there they wouldn't find in a Patience Strong poem or a therapist's column in a magazine. The Mystery becomes mundane.

The command to the Church is to go into the world and spread the word. I don't think it can do so by debasing that word. To a people who lived with mystery, as they did in Our Lord's day, the language of everyday was all that was needed if the message was to be understood. But now most of us live without consciousness of mystery, let alone sin, let alone redemption, let alone the prophesies; all we have left – if the message is to be even vaguely comprehended – is the resonance of language as it was used in the past. This seems to me the good argument, seldom used, against the debasement of meaning which we see in every attempt to make the Prayer Book open to understanding. But there is a real problem here: if there is to be one prayer book for all – if priest and congregation are to be at one level, as many – how do you communicate to everyone? "With this ring I thee wed" may seem short and simple and true – but to the literalist it does not: it's a puzzle, and most of today's population are literalists: a ring is a thing – the notion of symbol is not widely understood. Nor is anything abstract. (The word "guilty", for example, has to be translated to the person in the dock as "did you do what they're saying you did, or didn't you?") Better to ask people to say the words and leave the stage, than try to get down on all fours and see it from the Pram Service congregation's point of view (as we used to say, cynically, in advertising, of the client).

Chapter 12

Who should carry the can for failure?

Digby Anderson

Who is to blame for the failure of the Church of England? Or rather who should carry the can? For they are not quite the same question. Most modern organisations have a principle that the man at the top should get the praise when things go well and the blame when they don't. It does not necessarily mean that he, himself, actually caused the success or failure. It is partly that he is the symbol of the organisation, partly that his occupancy of the top denies the position to others who might do better.

Sometimes, of course, the leader will be more intimately associated with a particular policy and when it fails should obviously apologise and probably resign. Thus George Carey, as Archbishop of Canterbury, was closely associated with the Decade of Evangelism project. The project took up time and money. At the end of it the C of E had fewer members than at the beginning. It might be that it would have had even fewer members but that we cannot know. And the symbolic association of him with what looks like an expensive flop – and one many warned might be so – surely merits a quiet "I'm sorry".

Leaders should carry the can. But who leads the C of E? Historically the bishops do. The C of E is an episcopal church. The bishops inherit the authority and responsibility of the apostles. Some theologians will argue that this authority and responsibility cannot be sloughed off. The bishops are certainly entitled to recruit advisors and helpers and to involve others, but if they are bishops, then they retain responsibility. A grand exercise in involving others was what synodical government was. There are three houses of Synod, the clergy, the laity and the bishops. They all vote. I suppose a bishop might want to say that Synod is to blame for the C of E's failure. It is certainly an expensive, time-wasting bureaucracy. But those who have a high view of episcopacy will deny the bishops' ability to off-shoulder divinely given authority. And those who don't will note that the bishops still have one house and an influential one at that. Moreover, bishops in many senses have more power now than they did. The last decades have seen an enormous growth in the power and bureaucracy of the diocese – and of its expense. As with other organisations, bishops are not necessarily the proximate cause of each and every malfunction but they should carry the can.

What for? Well, the Gospels and Epistles and Credal and Conciliar documents of the universal church are pretty clear what bishops are responsible for. They are shepherds, pastors. Christ, the Good Shepherd says in John that he has not lost one of the apostles given to him by God the Father "save the son of perdition", Judas. "Feed my sheep", He orders the apostles (the bishops). Christ explains that every last one of the flock is to be watched, guarded and, if he wanders, brought back. Every last one must be kept and guarded because he has been bought at the price of Christ's blood. Indeed sometimes the shepherd must lay down his life for the sheep. There are other duties; he must hold firmly to sound doctrine. He must find new members. But the overwhelming obligation is to guard preciously every last person who is a member of the Church.

Most parish priests accept a variant of this and some are obsessed with it. When they take over a parish they know how many they have in their congregation and they worry enormously if they should lose someone, that is if someone leaves the church while under their care.

So what do the bishops do when church attendance plummets, when ordinations to the full-time ministry, church funerals, weddings and baptisms all fall? Do they apologise, resign or in any way carry the can? Usually what they do is to search desperately and find some ray of hope somewhere. I do not recall one case in the last 40 years when a bishop has blamed himself clearly and in public. How low must church attendance get before they do so?

And they ought to do more than apologise. For they have pursued policies, policies on a modern liturgy, on the ordination of women, on new translations of the Scriptures. And these policies have been justified, at least in part, by the idea that they will bring into the church or keep in it persons who are disaffected by its old-fashioned "irrelevant" ways. Well, they have not worked, these policies, so the apology should be accompanied by a re-think and perhaps a further apology to those who told them they never would work.

The Social Affairs Unit

Trustees:

Professor Julius Gould *Chairman*
John Greenwood *Treasurer*
Professor Anthony O'Hear
Frank Sharratt
Dame Barbara Shenfield

International Advisory Council:

Dr Alejandro Chafuen
Professor Christie Davies
Professor Adrian Furnham
Professor Jacques Garello
Professor Nathan Glazer
Dr Simon Green
Professor Leonard Liggio
Dr Theodore Malloch
Professor David Marsland
Professor David Martin
Professor Antonio Martino
Professor Kenneth Minogue
Professor Michael Novak
Professor Dennis O'Keeffe
John O'Sullivan
Dr Geoffrey Partington
Professor Erwin Scheuch
Dr Arthur Seldon CBE

Director: Dr Digby Anderson
Deputy Director: Michael Mosbacher

"The Social Affairs Unit is famous for driving its coach and horses through the liberal consensus, scattering intellectual picket lines as it goes. It is equally famous for raising questions which strike most people most of the time as too dangerous or too difficult to think about."

The Times

The Social Affairs Unit
Morley House
Regent Street
London W1B 5SA

www.socialaffairsunit.org.uk

Some publications from the Social Affairs Unit

NOT FIT TO FIGHT
The cultural subversion of the armed forces in Britain and America
Edited by Gerald Frost

The British armed services are threatened not by foreign powers but from within. If certain secular developments are forced on the necessarily different world of the military, then the forces will not be fit to fight.

COME BACK MISS NIGHTINGALE
Trends in professions today
Edited by Digby Anderson

The professions are threatened by anti-elitism, the cult of informality, managerialism and the loss of collegiality; above all, by the elevation of expertise over character.

OVERSPENDING IN THE NHS
An analysis by 5 doctors
Edited by Digby Anderson

It is conventional wisdom that the NHS is under-funded. But this conventional wisdom is wrong. The NHS may well have enough funds to meet essential demands if it stopped a large number of wasteful, inefficient and unnecessary treatments and practices.

THE DEATH OF HUMANE MEDICINE
And the rise of coercive healthism
Petr Skrabanek

"An astute critique of modern medical humbug... devastatingly accurate."
The Times